SNIPPETS

Edward Scarbrough

ISBN 979-8-89130-349-2 (paperback)
ISBN 979-8-89130-554-0 (hardcover)
ISBN 979-8-89130-350-8 (digital)

Christian Faith Publishing
832 Park Avenue
Meadville, PA 16335
www.christianfaithpublishing.com

Printed in the United States of America

Author's Note

I am ninety-two years of age. I have been married for sixty-nine years. We have two sons, ages sixty-five and sixty. I preached my first sermon in 1949, began my first pastorate in 1952. I dedicated my life to working with churches that needed help. In the process, I pastored four churches. One of them twice (between college and seminary); they called me back after seminary. Two of them I served for seven years each. One started with eighteen in attendance, and in seven years, we were averaging about 140. I taught in the public schools to support my family. I became a principal after about five years of teaching. I was the principal of a large high school. We had four assistant principals, and I was the administrative principal. For the last five years of my tenure, I served as regional director of the Academy of School Leaders for the State Department of Education. I have a master's degree in administration and supervision.

I have worked with churches in the Tri-Cities (Bristol, Kingsport, Johnson cities) for many years. Most of the churches where I served as interim pastor have asked me to be the interim at least three times. I tell you this to let you know that I take my work seriously.

I am no authority on sermon preparation, but I have been building sermons for at least seventy years. When I was active, I had what I called "My Seedbed." It was a loose-leaf notebook that I recorded any scripture that impressed my mind. I added to this as I studied and read. I prepared many sermons out of the seedbed.

I had to retire at about eighty years of age due to a heart attack. I had heart surgery and have a pacemaker. I maintain a study in my home and spend time every day studying Scripture. I got interested in the Letter to the Hebrews, so I worked my way through it. Then I began to record snippets that would lead to one or more sermons from each chapter. If someone can profit from my work, then I will be satisfied.

The Hebrew Letter

The Hebrew letter had a difficult time getting into the biblical canon. It was not until the fourth century that the letter was accepted, and then some scholars refused to accept it… including Martin Luther.

Some think it is a sermon or at least the framework of a sermon. It is a complex letter. It seems that some Christians were tempted to drift away from Christianity (2:1–3; 3:6; 12B; 4:1; 6:4–6; 10:26–39). They seemed to have suffered reproach, taunts, and criticism as Christians, so they were in danger of giving up their faith. The generally accepted theory is that they were tempted to go back to Judaism. The aim of the writer was to convince them of the superiority of Christianity over Judaism.

Many Bibles list Paul as the author. Few early church fathers held this view. Origen simply stated: "Only God knows who wrote it." Suggested authors include Barnabas, Apollo, Silas, Luke, Clement, Philip and Pricilla, and Aquila.

The quest for religion is unhindered fellowship with God. To gain this relationship requires an adequate knowledge of God. Jesus is the very image of God.

(Scriptures are from the New King James versions unless otherwise listed.)

Snippets from Chapter 1

God communicates with man. In times past, he spoke through prophets and angels. The messages come bit by bit. Only in Jesus do we have the full revelation of God. The prophets were considered to be in the secret council of God. "Surely, the Lord God does nothing unless he reveals his secrets to the prophets" (Amos 3:7). They were considered the voice of God to the nation.

However, they were limited by their humanity. They spoke out of their own personal experience. God has always used human personality in his work. No one prophet grasped the whole truth about God. Truth was fragmented until Jesus came and revealed the whole truth about God.

For example, Amos spoke about the social injustice of his day. He warned the people that unless they changed their ways, there would be disastrous results. Isaiah majored in the holiness of God to an unholy people. Hosea, out of his personal experience, spoke about the forgiveness of God.

The nation Israel placed great faith in prophets and angels. Angels were messengers of God. The context revealed whether it was a heavenly messenger or an earthly messenger. Either way the message was from God and was not to be ignored.

There came a time when God stopped speaking through prophets and angels and spoke through his Son. His Son was superior to prophets and angels because God himself validated his Son (Psalm 2:7; 45:6–7; 102:2). Jesus is the gateway to God. No one comes to the Father except through him.

This is a message highly disputed by our pluralistic society. Many feel they can ignore this truth. They chose personal freedom over biblical teaching. Ignoring Jesus is sowing to the wind and reaping the whirlwind. A good outcome requires a good input. You reap what you sow. To believe otherwise is whistling in the dark.

The Bible tells us, "Be sure your sins will find you out." It doesn't say they will be found out. No one may ever know. But our sins register in us. They will produce either good results or bad consequences.

When we put our trust in anything except the One who gave his life for us, we are trusting the wrong thing. God sent Jesus into this world to show us how to be saved from the things that destroy us.

The law of God

At first the nation followed the law. God gave Moses the law face-to-face, but the people believed so strongly in angels that they continued to believe God gave the law to angels and angels gave it to Moses ("who have received the law by the direction of angels" [Acts 7:53]. "It [the law] was appointed through angels by the hand of a mediator" [Galatians 3:9]).

God could have selected a legion of angels to work with him here on earth. He gave us the incredible honor of working with him in the kingdom here on earth. This honor came at a great cost.

We are stewards for God

God chose us to be his work companions. We are stewards. It is required of a steward that he be faithful. We can become lax in our stewardship. When the *Titanic* sank with the lives lost, the one who was assigned to be alert took off his headphones and left his post. His steamship was within twelve miles of the *Titanic* when it struck the iceberg. The radio operator on the steamship did not hate the people on the *Titanic*; he did not set out to deliberately let them die. He simply failed to do his duty. Our failure to be good stewards may result in catastrophic results.

Two different outcomes

When we come to the end of our lives, it matters greatly where our faith has taken us. Robert Ingersol, the brilliant agnostic, is an example of one who did not have faith in Jesus. He spent his time opposing *the way*. It is recorded that when he came to the end of his life, he muttered:

> Life is a narrow veil between two eternities. We strive in vain to look beyond the heights. We cry aloud, and the only answer is the echo of our wailing cry. (*The World's Best Orations*)

The other man is Paul. He spent his life telling people how to find the *way*. When he came to the end of his life, he said:

> I am persuaded that neither death nor life, nor angels, nor principalities, nor heights, nor depths, nor any other cre-

ated thing shall be able to separate us
from the love of God which is in Christ
Jesus our Lord. (Romans 8:38–39)

Snippets from Chapter 2

The author gives a brief warning: You must pay closer attention to the words you have heard to keep from drifting away from them. They came through angels, but they are still valid. If you ignore them, there will be consequences. If we do not hold onto the truth, we can easily drift into error.

The message now comes from Jesus. He has been crowned with glory and honor. Everything has been put under his authority. Since this is true, to ignore them will be of serious consequence.

The psalmist asked the question, "What is man that you are so concerned about him?" Is referencing man or the Son of man Jesus? Not all agree. In the original Psalm 8:4–6, he was talking about man in general, but the psalmist interpreted it to mean he was speaking about Jesus, the Messiah.

We do know that Jesus took it upon himself to come to earth in human form in order to identify with us. When things are not going well with us, Jesus knows what we are experiencing. He came to suffer what causes us to suffer, and his suffering was for us.

Frank Graeff, a Methodist minister, wrote a poem that turned into a song. The poem asks the question: "Does Jesus care when my heart is pained too deeply, so deeply that laughter is foreign to me?" He answers his question: "Oh yes, he cares. I know he cares. His heart is touched with my grief." We should not drift away from this kind of love.

We, too, are warned that if we ignore the message of Jesus, we may drift away from the truth.

We seldom plunge into error

We seldom plunge into error; we drift into it. Same with sin, we drift slowly into it. I have never had a person tell me that they intended to become addicted to alcohol or drugs. They drifted so slowly into the addiction that they became addicted before they were aware of their addiction.

This can happen to ministers. We can drift so slowly into error that we drift away from the truth. The tragedy here is that so many believe in us. We can poison the spring from which they drink.

Jesus told his disciples to "consider the lilies." This does not mean to just glance at them but study them with the purpose in mind to learn from them. We must give serious attention to the message from God lest we drift away from it. We sing, "Trust and obey for there is no other way." Trust means believe, and obey means we put into actions our belief.

There is a great truth in the Bible. The truth is that God so loved this world that he sent his Son to die for our sins. Why would anyone drift away from this love? The writer said he was made a little lower than the angels for a brief period of time. He experienced what we experienced.

It is hard for someone who is in robust health to really sympathize with the person who is battling serious health problems. Before we can enter into their suffering, we must walk in their shoes. The Bible makes it clear that Jesus walked where we walk and faced the same temptations we face but without sinning.

These temptations were real, or they were not temptations. So Jesus walked where we walk, and he knows our feelings. He suffered the same loneliness, the same sorrow, the same pain, the same fears, and the same doubts that plague us.

The two natures of Jesus

The two natures of Jesus (fully human and fully God) is one of the great mysteries of our faith. Here is where great faith is demanded. Jesus could have called a legion of angels to do his work, or he could have come as an angel, but then we would complain that he doesn't understand what we endure here on earth.

Another great truth

We must not drift from the truth that Jesus was true to his mission. We are to imitate his faithfulness to the task. Jesus began teaching his disciples as he walked with them. Before he ascended back to the Father, he commissioned us to continue his work. We must be found faithful to this task.

Conclusion

As Christians, we are salt and light in this world. Jesus didn't say we are to become salt and light but that we are salt and light. Salt and light must penetrate. Salt must penetrate food, and light must penetrate darkness.

As we walk through this world, we would like a light to shine into the future. But when we keep walking, we have enough light to lead us to our destination. I had this lesson brought home to me at a very early age. I would walk with my dad to visit his mother. It was usually dark, and she lived about a mile away. We took a lantern as light. A lantern produced a small circle of light that did not allow us to see in the distance. If we continued to walk in the light of the lantern, it was enough light to help us arrive safely at Grandma's house.

Snippets from Chapter 3

The author of the Hebrew letter again says that Jesus is superior. He has said that he is superior to the prophets and the angels. Now he says that Jesus is superior to Moses.

Moses held a unique place in the life of the Israelites. He is the only prophet that the Bible says God spoke with face-to-face. God gave him the law, and nothing was more important to the Israelites than the law.

In showing the superiority of Jesus to Moses, the author used the concept of a builder. God was the builder of the house. The world is God's house, and we are his children. The builder always receives more praise than the house.

Moses was faithful as a servant in the house of God (Numbers 12:7b). He was faithful in the management of all Israel's affairs. He was faithful, but he was not the builder. God was the builder. In a special way, Jesus is the builder of the church. We are God's house.

> I will build My church... (Matthew 16:18)

> Jesus is head of his church. (Ephesians 5:24)

> We are subject to him... (Ephesians 5:24)

Jesus came to earth and lived among us. He took on our humanity. God sent him on a mission, and he was faithful to his appointed mission. He is called "our apostle and High Priest." No other writer calls him "our apostle." The word "apostle" means "one sent." God sent his Son on a special mission to earth.

In the time of this writing, an apostle was an envoy of the religious high court of Israel. As a diplomat of the Sanhedrin, he had the full authority of the Supreme Court of Religion behind him. He was an ambassador of the Sanhedrin.

Jesus was God's ambassador to earth. When our country sends an ambassador to another country, they have the full authority to speak for America. Jesus is the voice of God to us.

He is our Great High Priest. The writer returns again and again to the idea of High Priest. The Latin term for priest is "bridge builder." Jesus bridges the gap between us and God. God is beyond our power to imagine.

> Isaiah said: "My thoughts are not your thoughts, nor are your ways my ways… for as the heavens are higher than the earth, so are my thoughts higher than your thoughts." (Isaiah 55:8–9)

Jesus let us see God, who is so high above us that it would be impossible to see or understand without him.

Since this is true, it is imperative that we not ignore him. To ignore him is to "harden the heart." This is a metaphor for ignoring the message of God. The reference is obviously to the incident in Exodus chapters seven through ten. In these chapters, God sends a message to Pharaoh: "Let my people go." Pharaoh ignored the message, and it says that he hardened his heart. After a time, it says that God hardened

Pharaoh's heart. This has become a problem for some. Most biblical scholars that I read do not believe that it was an arbitrary act on God's part. It was a step in his sovereign process of what had already happened. When Pharaoh continually ignored the message from God, he was allowed the freedom of hardening his heart. There seems to be no incident in the Bible where God hardened the heart of an innocent person simply to punish him.

Pharaoh's stubbornness was of such character that he was driven to the point of no return. Sadly, there seems to be a time limit on the patience of God. The Psalmist said:

> My people would not heed my voice…
> Israel would have none of me. So I gave
> them over to their own stubborn heart
> to walk in their own counsels. (Psalms
> 81:11–12)

When we continually ignore the message of God, we harden our hearts to some degree. This is a reality, not a scare tactic. Sin is so deceitful (13) that Satan tries to convince us that we have all the time we need. But we must "trust and obey." Trust is God's promise and act on this faith.

The nation Israel had a perfect example in their own history. They were led out of bondage and was being led to the land of promise. God provided for them, protected them, and answered their every plea. Yet they rebelled and even floated the idea that it would be better to return to slavery in Egypt. This unbelief caused them to wander for forty years in the wilderness. Moses led them out of Egypt, but because of their unbelief, he could not lead them into the promised land.

Today many refuse to heed the message of God. Politicians are using religion as a political ploy. An article in this week's *Johnson City Press* (January 2023) spoke to this very issue:

> Representative Jared Huffman of California, who identifies himself as a humanist, observed what many of his colleagues in Congress find to be politically useful. He says: "Many of them exploit a weaponized religion. They seem totally devoid from any authentic connection to the religion they weaponized."

This article surveyed the 118th congress and concluded: "Sadly politicians say what they want their constituents to hear."

Snippets from Chapter 4

How often have we said to our children, "I will do…I promise"? Promises made should be promises kept, but as parents, we break them. A broken promise brings disappointment and doubt.

God keeps his promises. He promised Israel a land, but the people failed to enter. God did not break his promise, Israel broke theirs. The message to Israel didn't do them any good because they did not believe God.

God has made a promise to save all who come to him. He will keep that promise. "The Lord is not slack concerning his promises…not desiring that any should perish" (1 Peter 3:9).

We are promised a "rest"

Perhaps at this point we need to look into the idea of rest. The author uses rest in two different ways. One way is rest from our earthly labors. When God finished his work of creation, he rested. This means that he ceased his creative work.

Israel was promised a rest. The land of promise was the rest they sought. There is a deeper spiritual concept of rest in this chapter. The author goes deeper than rest from earthly toil. He speaks metaphorically of God's offer of peace. He came to lift the burden of sin from our hearts. Our land of promise is heaven. *We* are going toward our land of promise, and those who have died have entered their rest, which is heaven (Revelation 14:13).

The promise is still valid (Hebrews 4:9). The author makes this very clear. "Take my yoke… Learn of me…and you will find rest for your soul" (Matthew 11:29).

Go down death

One of my favorite poems was written by James Weldon Johnson. It is a funeral oration about Sister Caroline. She is pictured, at first, resting from her earthly labors. "Take your rest… Take your rest." The best part comes when he speaks of her heavenly rest: "She is resting in the bosom of Jesus…" She has entered her "rest," which is heaven.

Nothing hidden

The Word will discover our readiness or our lack of readiness to enter our land of promise. If we hear the message and disregard it, we will not enter. Hearing is more than just listening. How many times have we said to our children: "Do you hear me?" Of course, they heard the sound of our voices, but what we meant was, "Do you hear me with the intent of doing what I am asking?"

I spent years as an interim pastor. I always ended my interim work with a message on "*How to Listen to a Sermon.*" Samuel Butler said it takes two to say a thing—a sayer and a sayee. The one is just as important as the other. We teach listening skills in our elementary grades because listening is so important. The same goes for the congregation of a church. We can listen and not hear with the intention of acting on what we hear.

Reaching our land of promise depends on how we hear. We cannot hoodwink God. He knows whether we intend to hear and act or hear and forget. When we hear that God knows us, what plays in the video of our minds? What emotions rise in our hearts—comfort or conflict? We must give an account of our lives to God (Hebrews 4:13b). Judgment is going on constantly in our lives. The slowness of the process of judgment throws many off. Jesus told a story about hearing and acting on what we hear.

Our Great High Priest

The author returns again to the idea that Jesus is our Great High Priest. He has entered his "rest," and there he intercedes for us. He understands our humanity…thus our weakness and our temptation. He was tempted like us but without giving in to the temptation.

Sometimes my temptation is because of my ignorance (lack of understanding). Jesus, on the other hand, was omniscient. This allowed him to see the outcome of events. This is comforting to me to know I can call on him in times of temptation and know that he knows what is in the future if I surrender to the pull of temptation.

We are warned again and again about ignoring the message from God. Each time we ignore the message, our hearts become a little harder.

William Russell was an English politician of the 1600s. He was accused of plotting the murder of King Charles II, along with his brother James, the duke of York. He was executed on July 21, 1683. It is reported that as he was being led to the scaffolds, he took out his pocket watch, handed it to a friend, and said, "I have no need of it. I am now dealing with eternity." Soon, we will all be dealing with eternity. "He that has an ear let him hear…"

Snippets from Chapter 5

The readers were obviously very familiar with priesthood. The High Priest was the chief officer of the Supreme Court of Religion. The Supreme Court functioned in the area of religion, morals, and politics. It had a varied history, but by the time of David, the status of priesthood was very high. No other class in Israel had a greater influence.

A go-between

The priest was the go-between man and God. He was a "bridge builder." He bridged the gap between man and God. He was a man appointed by God to represent the people. A man did not decide one day that he would be a priest. He was appointed to the mission. He was like other people, so he could understand their lives. He had the same weaknesses, the same temptations, and the same failings as others. This helped him have compassion for others.

His task was to offer the sacrifices and gifts that people brought to God. Because he was just a man, he had to offer a sacrifice for his own sin. Since he was no different from others, he would not be tempted to be unduly harsh toward them.

Even Jesus, our Great High Priest, did not seek to glorify himself. He glorified the Father, who sent him. The human side of Jesus shed tears, realizing that God was the only one who could save him from death. (5:7) He never tried to glorify himself.

He said: "I have glorified you (the Father)
on earth. (John 17:4)

He also said: "My food is to do the will
of him, who sent me, and to finish his
work. (John 4:34)

He finished the work God gave him to do and carried
our sins to the cross. He was the perfect sacrifice for sin. He
was made perfect by ascending back to the Father and seated
at his right hand, there to make intercession for us.

The writer abruptly turns his attention to the fact that
his readers had not grown in their spiritual lives. He had so
many things he needed to tell them, but they were dull in
their understanding. This dullness was due to their lack of
knowledge.

It is not easy to wrap our minds around spiritual things
when we have not grown in our spiritual lives. When we fail
to grow in spirit, then we are like infants, unable to discern
what is good and what is not. Growth is expected. Peter tells
us that the desire to grow must be there (1 Peter 2:2).

Just as the author compared the mission of Jesus to the
mission of an earthly priest, so we can compare the mission
of today's minister to the mission of the priest. God still calls
men to do his work here on earth.

John revealed the kind of person God calls:

There was a man sent from God… This
man came for a witness, to bear witness
to the light, that all through him might
believe. He was not that light but was
sent to bear witness of that light. (John
1:6–8)

So the minister is a *man*. I had this brought home to me as a student in seminary. Our New Testament professor was also pastor of a church. He said that one morning he did not have time to shave. The children always hugged him as they left the worship service. A father told him that on the way home, his daughter was unusually quiet. Suddenly, she asked, "Daddy, did you know that preachers have whiskers too?"

The minister is a man just like all men. He suffers the same disappointments, the same misunderstanding, the same doubts, and the same fears as all men. He is no different from others as far as life's experiences.

He is a man *sent from God*. Some might be tempted to say, "If he is a man just like me, why should I listen to him?" If he is a minister worth his salt, he has the calling of God on his life. He did not choose himself but was chosen for a mission.

His mission is to *bear witness to the light*. He does not preach his opinions but the truths of the Bible. He is under divine orders to know the Word and to be faithful to it. A witness does not make up a story and tell it, but he tells only what he knows from experience. Jesus calls himself "the light of the world" (1 John 1:5). The minister is bearing witness to that light.

As I write these words, we have just come through the season of lights—Christmas. Jesus came as light into a spiritually dark world. He is the light that lights the spiritual darkness. The minister is not that light but bears witness to that light. In the physical world, the moon has no light of its own; it merely reflects the light of the sun. The minister has no light of his own but reflects the light of the Son.

Ministers are expected to grow in the knowledge of the scriptures. You don't stop growing intellectually or spiritually just because you have completed a course of study. Continued education is required if you are able to be true to the Word.

Would you go to a doctor if he stopped growing in knowledge after finishing his residency? The doctor must keep growing in the latest techniques of surgery and the latest discovery of drugs that can impact certain diseases.

When we do not grow in our understanding of what it means to be Christian in action and attitudes, our behavior become more childish than childlike. We are to be children in spirit, not childish in behavior… There is a big difference.

Snippets from Chapter 6

What would your opinion be of a construction company that laid foundations but never built a structure on them? If the teacher has to continually go back over the basic principles, the student will never get the concepts that are necessary to higher learning.

The same is true in our Christian life. If it is necessary to continually cover the basic principles of Christianity, then the individual Christian will never reach the maturity demanded.

Growth is expected

The author mentions some of the elementary principles that we should have learned and gone beyond in our spiritual lives:

1) Repentance from dead works. We begin our journey of faith by changing our minds. We have a new attitude toward God, toward others, and even toward ourselves. Dead works would include deeds that bring death to the spirit.

2) Teaching about washings and baptism. Judaism had a lot of washings and even baptism. In the Christian experience, baptism is the entrance into

life. It is symbolic of dying to the old and rising to the new.

3) Laying on of hands was used to set apart for special services.

4) Resurrection from the dead. We are resurrected to walk in a new way now and will be resurrected to walk in a new way eternally.

What I hear in all these instructions is that we should strive to reach maturity in our spirit. "If any man have not the spirit of Christ, he is none of his." This is indication that I should be moving forward in my actions. The tragedy of failing to mature can lead to all kinds of problems.

Could it be that the problem the writer deals with came about because of their lack of maturity? The author compares our lives to the land. The land receives the sun and the rain, but some land produces only thorns and thistles.

The problem could stem from the fact that many Christians relate to their church the same way they relate to the stores in the mall. They approach it from the consumer angle. As a consumer member, if the church does not provide me with the services I want, then I simply look for another church. At times it is a simple as an athletic program for my children. Jesus made it clear that our role as disciples is participation with him in the work of the kingdom (John 14:12). We will be judged not on our athletic skills but on what our lives produce.

Impossible

In verses four through eight are some of the most difficult passages in the New Testament. We must assume that the first readers knew exactly what he was talking about. Was he speaking to those who were leaving Christianity to go back into Judaism? This seems reasonable since he mentions that they were crucifying Christ again.

Whatever he meant was that apostasy was a real possibility. He does not define "impossible." We need some logical answers, but I admit that I am just as confused as many who wrote on the subject.

One answer given was between those who hold a Calvinistic view and those who hold an Arminian view. The Calvinist say that once a person is born anew, he is eternally secure. The Arminian view is that we are eternally secure only if we endure to the end of life. Others simply leave it in the hands of God. He alone is capable of judging the human heart. Jesus told a story that relates to this; it is a story about seeds sown and the resulting crop. All the seeds were good but not all the soil was capable of producing good results. It all depended on the type of the soil. Seeds that landed on good soil produced a good crop. Was the point of this story the fact that some soils (lives) simply do not have the capacity to produce good results?

Almost immediately the author comforts his readers by assuring them that he does not believe they are in the impossible category. All of us have times when our faith is not as real as other times. But that does not mean we are in the impossible category. God is faithful and remembers our services as well as our failures.

God made a promise and sealed it with an oath. Abraham is a good example. God promised to bless the world through his linage. Time passed, and it seemed that God's promise would not come true. Both he and his wife, Sarah, were getting too old to have children. Would the promise fail? No, Isaac was born.

I stand with Abraham. Paul said it like this:

> He (Abraham) did not waver at the
> promises of God through unbelief but
> was strengthened in faith giving glory to
> God and being fully persuaded that what
> he promised he was also able to perform.
> (Romans 4:20–21)

God has given us the promise that all who come to him in faith will be saved.

Anchors of the soul

We have many anchors of the soul mentioned in the Bible.

"My sheep hear my voice, and I know them, and they follow me. I give them eternal life, and they shall never perish; neither shall anyone snatch them out of my hand. My Father, who gave them to me, is greater than all; and no one is able to snatch them out of my Father's hand." *This is an anchor of the soul.*

"I will never leave you or forsake you." *This is an anchor of the soul.*

"If you have faith in me, you will be saved." *This is an anchor of the soul.*

"I go to prepare a place for you." *This is an anchor of the soul.*

My conclusion, based on the promises of God, who does not lie, is that he will save us eternally if we come to God through him.

Snippets from Chapter 7

Melchizedek is a strange and mysterious character. In Genesis chapter fourteen, we have a brief mention of him, then he disappears from history.

Melchizedek

As Abraham was returning from battle, Melchizedek met him with bread and wine (sounds like a sacrament). He blessed Abraham. Abraham gave him a tenth of the booty from the battle. Nothing was said about his family history, his birth, or his death. Rabbis, arguing from what was not said, concluded that he did not die, that he is eternal.

The writer of the Hebrew letter makes a point to say how great Melchizedek was. He was greater than the father of the nation. It is assumed, but not told in Scripture, that he was not a member of the priestly tribe of Levi. In the law, you had to be a member of the tribe of Levi to be a priest. So a change in the law was demanded. He represented a new order of priest.

Jesus, our High Priest

Now we come to the reason for all of the above. Jesus is a priest of the new order. He was "made a priest after the order of Melchizedek." He was not a member of the tribe of Levi, but he is a legitimate priest.

The new order of priest is not approved on basis of linage or physical requirements (Lev 8). God chose Jesus to be our High Priest. Again, keep in mind that the purpose of religion is to introduce people to God. As our High Priest, Jesus can introduce us directly to God. The old order of priest had to pass on their task to another because they died. The word used here means that legally Jesus could not transfer his work to another. No one could replace him.

This is a great opportunity to speak about the cross. Here it tells us that Jesus offered himself as a sacrifice for sin. He did not have to offer a sacrifice for his own sin because he was without sin. He went as the Lamb of God and offered his blood rather than the blood of bulls and goats. He was not ashamed to take the bill of indictment against us and make a public display of it, nailing it to the cross. It said: "DEBT PAID IN FULL." It was based on his personal worth, not his human linage… *worthy is the Lamb.*

We act as representatives of God

"I came forth from the Father and have come into the world… Now I leave the world and go to the Father" (John 16:28). He told us that the Father had sent him; now he is sending us. We are not chosen on the basis of who we are. As representatives of God, we are to show the compassion of God. We do this with a listening ear, a loving heart, and witness of what it means to be Christian. Life if breaking down for many in our day. They need a human touch. We have a free choice—that's true—but we are not free to choose the result of our choice. The result is built into the choice.

The truth of this chapter jumps out at us. Jesus is called "the King of Peace." The one thing most desired today is peace. Peace does not come because of the absence of war. Peace comes when there is peace in the hearts of people. Christ offers us peace.

25

Snippets from Chapter 8

The author now turns from describing the priesthood after the order of Melchizedek to describing the priesthood after the One who is forever. It is founded on the personal greatness of Jesus, our Great High Priest. Death cannot touch his priesthood as it did the old one. In the old system, the priest had to be replaced and the sacrifice repeatedly made.

Jesus is the unique High Priest

Jesus is the unique example of divine majesty and divine service. Keeping in mind that the purpose of religion is to establish a relationship with God, Jesus does this very thing for us. In Christ, we have one who constantly intercedes for us before God. He does not die, and he offered a sacrifice once for us all.

A form

The old priesthood was just a copy of reality. Reality belonged to Jesus. The people of the old priesthood was living in the shadows of the real thing. The only reality is spiritual. Unfortunately, we have come to believe that the real is that which we can feel and touch. The Greeks had the idea that nothing material is real. For instance, the desk I am using at the present is a copy of the real thing. I can destroy this desk but not the idea of the desk.

The author is using language that we can understand. Only Jesus can lead us out of the shadows. The reality is spiritual. He can bring us before God as no earthly priest can do.

The need of a second

If the old system had solved the problem of the way to God, a second would not have been needed. Why search for a way that already answers the problem of our distance from God, not in miles but in relationship? Jesus said: "I am the way." He is the way to fellowship with God, and this way is the way of faith. The fellowship with God is spiritual. We come into this spiritual relationship by the way of "the new birth" (10).

We needed a new and better covenant. A covenant is an agreement between two parties. The terms are mutually agreed on, and if either party breaks the terms of the covenant, the covenant is void.

However, the writer switches to a different word here. He uses the word for "will." The terms of a will are made by the party creating the will. When we moved to Johnson City, we met with our lawyer and updated our will. The conditions of the will were made by my wife and me. No one can change them but us. We have two sons, who we love dearly, but they cannot change the will. They can either accept or reject the terms. A will is not made on equal terms like a covenant.

Our relationship with God is based on his terms. We can accept or we can reject them, but we cannot change them. Today many believe that they can change the way we must come into a relationship with God. They espouse many ways. But our ways are not God's way, and our thoughts are not God's thoughts.

The old covenant, which Israel agreed to, is found in Exodus 24:1–8. But a new one was promised (Jeremiah 31:31–34). This new one is based solely on the will of God and solely on his love and grace. It is revolutionary but promised by the God who keeps promises. It is universal in scope. All people can now come to God and have a personal relationship with him, but we come on his terms and not ours. The new is not written on tablets of stone but is written on the hearts and minds of people. Before Jesus left this earth, he told his disciples (and all of us) that his Spirit would be here to indwell and lead us.

Conclusion

We now have a way prepared for us to come into this relationship with God. The Holy Spirit is our guide. Jesus made a sacrifice for our sins. We no longer depend on the blood of bulls and goats. They could remind but they could not save. We now can come personally with boldness to God. *The way has been made for us all.*

Snippets from Chapter 9

This chapter concludes the writer's proof that Jesus is superior to the earthly priesthood. He now proceeds to contrast the ministry of the old with the new. It is obvious from verses one through five that the sanctuary cannot cleanse the conscience or provide real access to God.

Aids to worship should never become objects of worship. The Holy Spirit used the physical to teach about the spiritual. The blood of bulls and goats speak of a higher cleansing. We need a cleansing of the conscience, not just the cleansing of the outer person.

The coming of Christ into history changed our understanding of God. Jesus said that if we have seen him, then we have seen God. He gave us a picture of what God was like. He also came to do what the old system of sacrifice could not do, bring us into the presence of God.

The author said that the earthly sanctuary was a copy of the heavenly sanctuary. Jesus was the real sacrifice for sins. He died once and for all. He opened the way to God. We can now come boldly before the throne.

Under the old, a man could serve as priest for a lifetime without coming into the presence of God. God symbolically dwelt in the holy of holies, but only the High Priest could go in and once a year. This shows that Judaism had not solved the problem of religion, which was to bring us into a personal relationship with God.

The curtain

A curtain separated the average person from God. It is significant that at the cross, the curtain in the temple was torn from top to bottom. This means that God had opened the way to his presence. If the curtain has been torn by man, it would have been torn from bottom to top. The splitting of the curtain speaks volumes. God is no longer unapproachable. This proves that Christianity is superior to Judaism.

The will

A strange thing happened in the middle of the discussion of the covenant relationship between man and God. The writer switched to a word that means "will" rather than covenant. A covenant is an agreement between two parties. A will is made by one person, and the terms are carried out upon his death.

The implication is that Christ's death was necessary in the order that the heavenly inheritance might be ours (9:11–17). The will of Christ is that all people be saved (2 Peter 3:9). The death of Christ gave us the gift of forgiveness of sin and life everlasting.

The cross

The cross speaks of physical suffering and spiritual isolation. At the cross, we hear the jeering mod, the clicking of dice, the cursing of soldiers. We see the dried blood, the swarming flies, and the human degradation. A human body hanging naked for every eye to see. This was the intent of Rome. It was their way of saying, "Break our law and this is what will happen to you." On the emotional level, it is difficult for us to comprehend.

How could one human being be so cruel to another human being?

But when Jesus shed his blood for us, the basic question was answered. "How can I, a sinner, come into a personal relationship with a holy God?" Then I remember that it is not physical distance but relationship that separates us. Christ shed his blood to close the gap.

A great opportunity

The opportunity to speak about the cross is in this chapter. It speaks clearly about Christ shedding his blood for the sins of the world. The cross tells me that forgiveness is never easy. It is not easy for us, and it was not easy for God. We hear so much about forgiveness that we get the idea that all God has to do is snap his finger, and presto, we are forgiven. But the cross tells us another story.

Forgiveness is essential to life both physically and spiritually. We must forgive those who wrong us, not only because they need it but because the only key to a personal prison is forgiveness. Forgiveness is so important that Jesus said when we come to worship and they remember that there is someone who needs our forgiveness, leave the worship experience, go and make it right with that person, then come back and worship. If Jesus thought it so important, then I best remember.

A story in *USA Today*, September 20, 2007, told the story of a man who died protecting his fellow soldiers by throwing himself to an explosion. The lead story was about five men in a Humvee in Iraq. It told of their personal struggle to come to grips with the heroic act of a fellow soldier. A grenade was hurled into the Humvee... Immediately, Ross McGinnis dropped down on the grenade and was killed.

The thing that struck me was that all the men were having difficulty emotionally, comprehending why someone would do such a thing. I cut the article out and filled it because it spoke to me about the death of Christ. The most profound thing in this world is why Christ took it upon himself to die for my sins. He took my pain, my suffering, my sins and nailed them to the cross. Paul expressed it like this: "Having wiped out the handwriting of requirements against us… He has taken it out of the way, nailing it to a cross" (Colossians 2:14).

Snippets from Chapter 10

The author is nearing the close of his formal argument. He goes back to some points that he already touched on but adds much that are new.

I repeat that the business of religion is to bring us into a relationship with God. We begin this relationship when we are born anew. The best the old system could do is give people a distant relationship with God. He was symbolically enclosed behind a curtain.

The old system reminded people of sin

The fact that the sacrifice had to be repeated over and over proved that it did not erase sin. All it did was remind them that sin still needed to be confessed and paid for by the blood of animals. "These yearly sacrifices reminded them of their disobedience and guilt, instead of relieving their minds" (Verse 3, Living Bible).

These over and over sacrifices simply reminded them of their guilt. They needed release from sin but could not find it in the old system. The old system is a "shadow" or copy of the real, the heavenly sanctuary. As Christians, we need to be aware that we could be guilty of a similar problem. When we continually pray about some egregious sin in our life without accepting God's forgiveness, we simply bring it to mind over and over.

The author puts the words of Psalm 40 into the mouth of Jesus. Obedience has always been the gateway to God. "To obey is better than sacrifice and to heed is better than the fat of rams" (1 Samuel 15:22).

The old system could not save

The old system of sacrifice could not save regardless of the number of times it is repeated. The sacrifice of Christ is the only blood that could cleanse the heart. Christ came into history to do what the blood of animals could not do. The animals that were sacrificed had no consciousness of the sin of the people nor did they die a voluntary death. Christ came to do what the death of an animal could not do, forgive sin. He became man in order to sympathize with us but also so that he could offer himself for sin. He who gives his life as a sacrifice for sin must first be one of us.

Christ on the cross and the resurrected Lord can change us. This is what repentance means—a change of mind, a change of heart, and a change of direction. As we witness, we must take care not to leave the impression that we will not like them unless they change. The way God changes us is to let us know that he loves us and wants a better life for us. He wants us to change not so he can love us, but so we can become all that we are designed to be.

The good news is that he is in the heavenly sanctuary being mediator for us. Whereas the High Priest could go into the holy of holies (the presence of God) once a year, Christ is forever in the presence of God.

Practical implications

The author turns to the practical implications of what he has been saying about Christ. When Christ died, the curtain that separated God from the people was torn, signifying that the way to God has been opened. We can come boldly into his presence. Since Jesus has opened the way to God, we should draw near to him.

Another practical application—we need one another. Jesus established the church as a way for us to find fellowship and strength with others. The world is full of discouragers. We are to be encouragers. We find courage and strength in the fellowship of other believers. One of the duties of Christians is support of others. We all go through times when we need more strength than we can muster. We sing: "Before our Father's throne, we pour out ardent prayers. Our fears, our hopes, our aims are one, our comfort and our cares."

When this is more than a song that we sing, when it is reality, we can overcome our problems. When we fail to support one another, we fail our responsibilities. It is easy to drift into a selfish kind of life. This is a contradiction of all that Jesus said should characterize our lives. Why do some neglect the gathering together? Could it be that they do not feel others understand what they are experiencing?

A dire fate

People who deliberately reject God reject the only sacrifice that there is for sin. The alternative is judgment of God. The author asked: "If those who broke the law were given no pity, what will happen to those who trample the Son of God under foot?" There is a solemn warning that if we reject the sacrifice of Christ, there remains no other. Apostasy was a deliberate choice. It means you are aligning yourself with those who put Christ on the cross.

"It is a fearful thing to fall into the hands of an angry God." This startling statement turned my mind immediately to Jonathan Edwards. He preached a sermon on this subject on July 8, 1741, and it still lives in our minds. Historians tell us that during the preaching of the sermon, the congregation groaned and shrieked. A brother in the congregation was not able to restrain himself and called out, "Mr. Edwards, Mr. Edwards, is not God merciful too?" It is reported that the dying words of Mr. Edwards were, "Trust God and ye need have no fear" (*The World's Best Orations*).

Yes, God is merciful too.

God is merciful. (Psalm 61:1)

Trust in the mercy of God forever. (Psalm 57:8)

And God who is rich in mercy, because of his great love with which he loved us... (Ephesians 2:4)

God's mercy means he does not give us what we deserve. God's grace means he gives us what we do not deserve.

Remember

We are asked to remember. Remember how you kept your faith alive while going through suffering. Perhaps if we remember the end of it all, then we would have the heart to continue to be faithful. Just keep doing the will of God, and this will assure your relationship with God.

The church at Ephesus was asked to remember what it was like when they first came into Christ. Restore this first love. The author says that the Lord is coming soon. This is a good time to preach on the second appearing of Christ.

Snippets from Chapter 11

The author encourages the readers to stand firm in faith. Faith can lift us to fellowship with the unseen God. While we live in this world, faith can carry us to the heavenly sanctuary. Faith can help us experience the future in the present.

The author probably did not intend to give us a formal definition of faith but to simply single those parts of faith he wished to bring to our attention. We live our lives by faith.

> Now faith is the substance of things hoped for, the evidence of things not seen. (Hebrews 11:1 NKJV)

> Now faith is the assurance of things hoped for, the proof of the reality of things we cannot see. (Hebrews 11:1 Williams Translation)

We will look at some of the possibilities for messages in this chapter. It lends itself to multiple sermons, beginning with the biography of those he mentions.

Abel: The Bible tells us that God accepted the offering of Abel but not the offering of Cain. It does not tell us why this happened. There are so many guesses, but they are just that—guesses. Abel is pictured as a martyr for righteousness (Matthew 23:35).

Since we are not told why God did not accept the offering of Cain, we need to focus on the offering of Abel. He evidently gave serious thought to what he brought as a gift to God.

We need to give serious thought to what we bring to God. When we think of offering, we usually think in monetary terms. There are things more valuable to the kingdom of God than money. Time is valuable. It has more value today than money. There are so many demands on our time that we fail to give time to the important things.

Our abilities is another gift that we can bring to God. Our abilities are given to us by God, and we are to use them to help advance the kingdom of God on earth. Paul said that we are his workmanship created to do good works. We are to be like a good timepiece. It is created to do one thing, keep time. We were created to do good works in God's kingdom here on earth. Abel still speaks to us by means of his faith. Even though he is dead, his faith still encourages us. We should remember that our faith can inspire others, even after we leave this earth.

Enoch: Enoch is the elder son of Cain (Genesis 4:17). The event we remember most is that the Bible says: "He was not found…" This is a quote from the Greek version of the Old Testament. The translators added the words "not found." The Hebrew text simply states that he "was not." This has led to great speculation. Before he was taken up, it says, "He pleased God." His faith was obviously the reason he was taken up.

It also says, "he walked with God." When we walk with someone, it means we have the destination in mind. We usually walk with a friend. While walking, we share information. It is important that while we are here on earth that we walk with God. When we leave this world, we will continue to walk with him.

Noah: It took a great faith for Noah to believe God when he had no evidence of a future flood. He must have endured the taunts and skepticism of neighbors. Our faith may lead us into paths that others do not understand. Noah simply listened to others but continued to build a large boat. His faith saved the animals that were important in rebuilding the world after the flood. At times our faith may be misunderstood by even our family, but we are to walk by faith. The gospel itself is foolishness to many, but it is the power of God to people of faith. There is an old T-Shirt that on the front said: "I am a fool for Christ." On the back it read, "Whose fool are you?"

Jacob: Even with all his failings, God still had a plan in mind for Jacob. His life was so confusing that it was hard to see how God could use him, yet he finally encountered God. This encounter with God was real and lifechanging. One night on a lonely road, he met God, and his life was never the same.

He left his home because of his cheating. But God had promised to bring him back. Jacob's life is a testimony to what God can do when we are willing to work with him. The story of Jacob is so big that many messages can be preached from it.

Joseph: Joseph is a man whose life speaks to all of us. It took great faith to believe that God was involved in the happenings of his life. He was hated by his brothers, sold into slavery, lied about, and imprisoned. But by faith, he went from prison to second-in-command in one of the greatest nations on earth at the time.

Here is a man whose faith shows like a beacon. When his brothers were thinking about how they would be treated by this brother, he showed his faith in God by telling them, "It was not you who sent me here but God" (Genesis 45:8). He, of all the sons of Jacob, was given a position in the Genesis story alongside of the great fathers of the nation.

Abraham: The story of Abraham is a story of a man who shows great faith. He is the father of the Hebrew nation (Matthew 3:9). He was asked to leave his hometown and go to a land he did not know. His trials were well-documented by those who attended Bible study.

It was by faith that he believed God when he was chosen to be a blessing to the whole world. It was by faith that he believed God when he was told he would have a son. At the time, both he and Sarah were well past childbearing years. Then it took great faith when God told him to sacrifice his promised son. This was the crowning test of his faith. He believed that if he killed his son that God could bring him back to life.

Sarah: Sarah laughed when she was told she would have a son. She was past the age of childbearing. She did not doubt that God would keep his promise. Her faith caused Isaiah to call her "the mother of Israel" (Isaiah 51:2).

Moses: Moses is associated with the story in the book of Exodus. He is noted for what he was but also for what he became in the hearts of a nation.

It took great faith for his parents to defy the Pharaoh's orders to kill all Hebrew boys at birth. His mother placed him where he would be found by the daughter of the Pharaoh. He grew up as the son of the daughter of the Pharaoh. He enjoyed all the advantages of the king's court. His faith never let him forget who he was. It took a great faith for him to refuse to be called the son of the Pharaoh's daughter. This meant suffering with the nation of slaves rather than enjoying the pleasures of Egypt.

Let me interject something at this point. I have heard a lot of preaching that sin has no pleasures, but sin provides many pleasures. Sin offers the quickest way to getting rich; it offers many sensual pleasures. You don't have to worry about the feelings of others, etc. Sin offers many pleasures, but in reality, they are "passing pleasures." Sin always offers more than it can deliver.

It took great faith for Moses to forsake Egypt and return to lead a nation to freedom. The task of leading them out of Egypt was difficult, but a greater task lay ahead. He had to lead them for forty years while wandering around in the wilderness, complaining about their condition.

It took a great faith for him to believe that God could rescue them when trapped between an army and the sea.

The final scene came when he was summonsed to Mt. Nebo. He, with all his labor, was not able to lead them in the land of promise. But the obedience of Moses, throughout his life, is evident in all the story. It took a great faith, but Moses was able to maintain his faith even when he was not allowed to enter the land promised by God.

The important point made by the author of Hebrews is that all these heroes of faith died before realizing the promise of God. *This is a great message for us.*

Introduction to Snippets on Faith

Faith is not a psychological bootstrap but a reality. Some spend too much time rehearsing their uncertainties when they need to spend time rehearsing their faith.

Ask God to guard your mind. "The peace of God... will guard *your mind*" (Philippians 4:7). Paul told young Timothy: "God does not give us the spirit of fear but...a *sound mind*" (2 Timothy 1:7). If fear is the answer to our questions about the here and now as well as the future, then Snoopy's (a dog in the comic strip) advice is relevant: "There is no sense in a lot of barking if you really don't have anything to say."

God told Moses, as he was leading the nation Israel out of Egypt with Pharaoh's army coming up from the rear and a sea facing them, "Stop being afraid... Stand still and see what God can do" (Exodus 14:13).

Let me paraphrase: "Stop doubting, stand still, and have faith in Jesus Christ as Lord and see what God can do."

Snippets on Faith

Without faith it is impossible to please God

Faith in the Bible

The Bible is a unique book. It is God's word to us, but it came through men like us. Man was the medium, but God was the author. "Prophecy never came by the will of man but holy men of God who spoke as they were moved by the Holy Spirit."

Jesus confirmed the scriptures. "Have you not read the scriptures? The stone which the builders rejected has become the chief cornerstone" (Mark 12:10). He was quoting Psalm 118:22–23. He confirmed the scriptures in many places by quoting them.

Paul could say with complete confidence, "All scripture is given by inspiration of God and is profitable for doctrine, for proof, for correction, for instruction in righteousness" (1 Timothy 3:16).

What a great time to preach on the creation story from Genesis. There is a great debate on how the creation of this universe came into being. Science and religion have many theories, but they are just that, theories. Neither science nor religion can *prove* how it all began.

Christianity is based on faith. Genesis has a lot to say about creation, but when all is said and done, it simply means

God did it. Several times in the creation story, we read, "and God said…and it was." The author of Hebrews stated it best: "By faith we understand that the world was framed by the Word of God."

It serves no useful purpose for us to argue about how it all began. It is all of faith. Only a great faith can accept the astonishing news that "the things which are seen were not made of things which are visible." Faith says, "God spoke and the worlds came into existence." If we don't have faith in the Bible, how can we have faith in what we preach?

Faith in the cross

The cross is central to our faith. All four of the gospel writers tell of the cross (Matthew 27:32–50; Mark 15:22–32; Luke 23:26–45; John 19:18–24).

Believe that only through the sacrifice of Christ can we find the meaning of our existence and our hope for eternity for many is beyond their power to comprehend. But faith did not originate in an idea of God but an act of God. The cross is something visible, something concrete, and something historic.

Faith in the cross means faith in the Christ of the cross. The physical cross was cruel beyond our minds to comprehend. It meant suffering, anguish, mockery, and humiliation. The crucified hung naked for every eye to see. Rome meant it this way. They wanted to leave the message, "Violate our laws and this is your destiny."

There were three crucified that day. On one hung the Son of God. He suffered and died for our sins. Paul said, "He humbled himself and became obedient to the point of death, even the death of the cross" (Philippians 2:8).

The message of the cross is foolishness to those who are perishing, but to those of us who are being saved, it is the wisdom and power of God. The way to a relationship with God is the way of the cross.

The cross touches us at the deepest level of our being. It is love personified. The only solution to the problems of hate in this world is the love of God. Force cannot ultimately change people. It can subdue for a time but cannot conquer the heart. You can't make living things grow by the use of a sledgehammer; it matters not how hard you pound. Every thinking parent knows this, every school teacher knows this, and the sooner we learn it as a people, the better off we will be. Change comes about when the heart is changed.

The message of the cross is too big for one sermon. Multiple messages are needed.

Faith in Forgiveness

There is nothing man wants to know more than to know that he is forgiven for his sins. Yet with all the scriptures that tell us about forgiveness, people still doubt it. It is an emotion that is hard to conquer.

Why do we have such a hard time believing that God has forgiven us when we confess and forsake our sin? We tend to confess the same sin over and over, thus doubting that God has forgiven us.

We have God's promise.

> And you, being dead in your sins…he has made alive together with him, having forgiven all your trespasses. (Colossians 2:13)

> In him, we have redemption through his blood, the forgiveness of sin. (Ephesians 1:7)

> Repentance and remission (act of forgiveness) of sins should be preached in his name. (Luke 24:47)

On and on we could go, but these are typical of the scriptures on forgiveness.

There are some requirements on our part: we must confess and forsake. We have to forsake our hate, our revenge, our greed, and such in order to enjoy the forgiveness of God. Forgiveness is not given in isolation. Jesus taught in the Model Prayer: "Forgive us our sins for we also forgive everyone who is indebted to us."

Jesus is not advocating a one-to-one relationship to God forgiving when we forgive others. The truth of the matter is that we are not open to God's forgiveness when we refuse to forgive others.

Forgiveness is essential

Forgiveness is essential to peace of mind. It is as essential to our emotional health as food is to our physical health. When Jesus taught us to pray "Give us this day our daily bread," he was teaching us that forgiveness, and bread are two essentials of life.

As we approach the end of life here on earth, forgiveness takes on a whole new meaning. The certainty of forgiveness takes the fear out of dying. It does not take the dread of leaving our loved one here, but the fear is gone. We have faith that God keeps his promises.

Jesus did not leave us unclear of what real forgiveness requires. In John chapter eight, there is an incident in the life of Jesus where forgiveness was needed. Everyone in the story needed forgiveness. Each was battling their own sins. "Which of you is without sin can cast the first stone."

Matthew chapter eighteen reveals just how seriously Jesus looked on forgiveness. Simon Peter felt he was being liberal in his reasoning: "Lord, how often shall my brother sin against me and I forgive him? Seven times?"

"No," said Jesus, "not seven times but seventy times seven."

Three ideas that need to be developed into messages:

1) We must forgive ourselves in order to be able to forgive others.
2) If God forgives my sin and remembers it no more, why should I confess it over and over?
3) Forgiveness is often confused with condoning sin but not so. Forgiveness is dealing with the sinner, not the sin.

Faith in the present

Too many today have little hope for the present. They live their lives without hope. Circumstance does challenge our faith. Paul, writing the Christians in Corinth, spoke of the "present distress" (1 Corinthians 7:26). Every generation faces challenges.

The first-century Christians faced a danger unlike any we have experienced. They lost their jobs because of their faith. They lost their standing in the community. In fact, they lost almost everything. Yet they did not lose their hope in the present. Paul expressed what they felt in a letter to the Christians in Rome: "I do not consider that the sufferings of the present time…worthy to be compared with the glory which shall be revealed in us" (Romans 8:18).

Circumstance did not weigh the first-century church down but picked them up. They turned the world right side up because of their faith.

There is no question that our present time is a danger-ous time. Nations are threatening nations. Nuclear buildup is threatening to end it all in a nuclear haze. Many nations, who have the power and capability to create dangerous times, do not recognize God.

These are great times for us to express our faith in God. Jesus said that the peacemakers would be happy. He did not say "peacekeepers" but "peacemakers." You can keep the peace using physical force, but you cannot create peace. The only thing that will bring peace to the present is for us to have peace in our hearts.

At times we feel like Job in the Old Testament. "My days are spent without hope" (Job 7:6). When this is true of us, we need to remember that "Christ in you, the hope of glory" (Colossians 1:27). "We are more than conquerors through him who loved us" (Romans 8:34).

Faith in the future

Faith in the future rests on faith in the present. If you do not have faith in the present, you have no future. For a Christian, it is encouraging to know that "Jesus is the same yesterday, today, and forever" (Hebrew 13:8).

Common sense tells us that we are destroying our future. Our natural resources have an uncertain future. The rattling of nuclear swords leave us cold. Water is now a crisis. The Mississippi River is so low that barges have a difficult time navigating. Much of our food supply move up and down this river. The Colorado River, which supplies water to millions, is becoming unable to meet the demands. Water is as important as air to sustain life. Now they tell us that AI could spell the end of civilization.

Looking at events logically, we do not see much hope. For the Christian, our hope is not in this world. This is not "pie in the sky" but reality. Our future extends all the way to eternity. "If in this life only we have hope…we are of all men most pitiable" (1 Corinthians 15:19).

Despair breeds despair; faith breeds faith. Faith builds a bridge over the chasm of despair. This world is not our destination. Our hope is in Christ. He told us that he was going to prepare a place for us. The old song was right: "This world is not my home. I'm just passing through."

Jesus left us with this great commission: "Go into all the world and make disciples, and going *I am with you*, even until the end of the age."

This promise covers the present and the future.

Faith in prayer

I believe in communication with God—prayer. This may seem strange to some, but I have a problem with public prayer. How could a man who has spent a lifetime working with churches and who has prayed many a public prayer have a problem with public prayer?

It is my problem and mine only. The problem I have is a minister can slip into praying to the congregation when he is supposed to be leading them in communication with God. You have to be very careful, or you will be making a point to the congregation rather than speaking to God. There have been times when I have listened to public prayer and wondered, *To whom is he talking?*

Jesus indulged in praying in a public place (when blessing children, healing, etc.) but no recording of him engaging in planned public prayers.

The one place that we cannot be false is in our private place. In Matthew, he said: "But you, when you pray, go into your room, and when you have shut the door, pray to your Father who is in secret, and your Father who sees in secret will reward you openly'.' In our private room, we cannot hoodwink God. He knows the motivation of our heart.

Now let's get to faith in prayer. We must believe that God hears and answers our prayers. The psalmist had this assurance. "Lord, you have heard the desires of the humble"

(Psalms 10:13). Prayer is communication with God. We tell God the desires of our hearts, and we listen for God to talk to us in that still, small inner voice.

Faith in prayer is essential. We must believe that God hears, or we are just talking to ourselves.

Faith in the church

We are the church. When we say, "I am going down to the church," most think it means "I am going down to the buildings." Our forefather had it right; they said: "I am going to the meetinghouse." When Paul was writing to "the church at…" he was writing to the people. So when people say they have lost faith in the church, it means they have lost faith in us.

The organized church is going through some difficult times. Almost daily, the news media tells another story of some church body in trouble. So people are leaving the organized body because they have lost faith in the members.

One of our problems is that we have become a congregation of listeners rather than a congregation of doers. Jesus said we are to be salt and light to the world. Salt and light must penetrate to be effective. Salt must penetrate food, and light must penetrate the darkness. Salt can lose its saltiness, and light can be hidden under a bushel.

I have spent seventy years working with churches, which means working with people. There was a time when we taught people how to win others to have faith in Christ. This almost never happens now.

Jesus loves the people, meaning he loves the church and gives himself for us. We have a great responsibility. Jesus said that when people have a problem, they should take it to the church. We don't solve many problems today.

Here is how he defined his mission:

> The Spirit of the Lord is upon me because
> he has anointed me to preach the gospel
> to the poor, he has sent me to heal the
> brokenhearted, to preach deliverance to
> the captives and the recovery of sight to
> the blind, to set at liberty those who are
> oppressed and to preach the acceptable
> year of the Lord.

I remember something else; he said: "As the Father has sent me, I am sending you" (John 20:21).

I firmly believe that when we recover our mission, we will recover those who we have lost.

Conclusion

The heroes of faith all died before they realized the promises of God. They did not spend time arguing about the value of faith but encouraged us to hold on to faith. When we keep the faith, we are "more than conquerors through him who loved us."

But this relationship requires maintenance. If we ignore our friends, do not keep in touch, do not help in times of trouble, and simply avoid them. How long will we be able to maintain this friendship?

Same is true with our faith. Our relationship with God requires maintenance, such as prayer (talking with him), worship (letting him talk to us), and witness (sharing our faith with others).

Faith that sustains includes faith in the Bible, faith in the cross, faith in forgiveness, faith in prayer, faith in the church, faith in the present, and faith in the future.

Snippets from Chapter 12

The Christian life is compared to a race. In the grandstands are family, friends, and neighbors. They are there to cheer us on. We want to win the race, but we also do not want to disappoint those who came to cheer for us. Verses one and two are some of the greatest verses in the New Testament. If we cannot preach a message to them, then our wood is wet.

In the grandstands are our heroes of faith. Jesus, our supreme example of faith, is there cheering for us. People in the stands are essential to the game. During the Covid pandemic, teams played before empty stadiums and empty courts. The games were called "ghost games." Players said that it was difficult to get up for these games because of the lack of people in the stands.

We all get discouraged in the race of life. The author encourages us not to grow weary or discouraged. When we do get this way, we need to turn our eyes toward Jesus. He did not give up because of the cross. He faced the disgrace of dying as a criminal because he knew what awaited. He is now seated at the right hand of the throne of God.

Paul uses the picture of an athletic event to get the point across:

> Everyone who competes for a prize is temperate in all things... They do this to obtain a perishable crown, but we are

imperishable. Therefore, I run thus not
with uncertainty. Thus I fight: not as one
who beats the air. But I discipline my
body and bring it into subjection lest,
when I have preached to others, I myself
should be disqualified. (1 Corinthians
9:25–27)

In another letter, he tells us that a soldier does not allow
himself civilian pursuits not because they are wrong but
because he has committed himself to the military. It seems
the church at Corinth was forgetting to whom they were to
be committed. They were going their own way, refusing to
sacrifice self in order to help others. Paul reminded them
that "all things are lawful, but all things are not helpful" (1
Corinthians 10:23). What he was saying to them was "Don't
just think of what you want but consider how you will appear
to others."

God, a loving Father

When we think of God, we are to think of him as a
loving Father. Jesus told us that when we pray, we are to recognize God as "our Father who is in heaven."

An earthly father who does not correct his children
has no regard for their future. A father should be concerned
about the highest good for his children. He is concerned
about their present and their future. We discipline our children out of a fallible judgment, but God disciplines us with
the knowledge of our future already in mind.

When my dad told me that "this will hurt me more
than it hurts you," I did not believe him. When I had sons
of my own, I realized what he said was true. Because of a
question from a son, I took the time and effort to write the

story of my life as I remembered it. I wanted them to know that their dad is better. In this autobiography, I told them: "Any mistakes we made as parents were mistakes of the head and not of the heart." We disciplined because we loved them.

Weary and discouraged

The witnesses mentioned here all died before realizing the promises of God, but they continued in faith. Remember that Jesus is cheering us on. We can become discouraged in life. This is human, but we need to look to the witnesses in our lives who continued even when discouraged.

A great responsibility

One of the great responsibilities that is ours involves others. The author is talking to the church here. He tells them to "lift up feeble hands, keep walking, try to live in peace, take care that bitterness does not take root, and don't be like Esau who had no spiritual depth and no faith." We are to live our lives with conscience of our impact on other people. We should not allow things to become more important than people.

"See that you do not refuse him who speaks" (Hebrews 12:25). If those who ignored the message of the prophets were judged harshly, how much more harshly will we be judged who ignore the message of God's Son?

He speaks of the heavens and the earth shaking. Applying this to our time is easy because we are living in shaking times. People blame the government for the shaking times. Republicans blame Democrats, and Democrats blame Republicans. Others blame the Communists or the atheists. *But what if it is God doing the shaking?* Maybe he is shaking our times that the temporary things may be shaken down for the eternal things to be revealed.

We have a kingdom that cannot be shaken or destroyed. Jesus said that he would build his church, and the gates of hell could not overcome it. We have faith that God still controls this world, and perilous times require a great faith and a holy fear. The only things that will remain are the spiritual.

Snippets from Chapter 13

The author now deals with the practical side of Christianity. He asks the readers to patiently listen to what he has been saying, then he gives some practical things that should characterize the life of a follower of Christ.

Keep loving one another

Mutual love is a dominant characteristic of the Christian life. Love is more than an emotion; it is an action. It is wanting the best for the one we love. The early church loved one another, and it drew the attention of the nonChristian world. Love identifies us as children of God.

John makes a case for love that we must not overlook (1 John 4:7–11). We, at times, do not take love seriously enough. He basically tells us that love comes from God, and if we are his children, we will show this love to others. This is proof that we are children of God.

We are not left to figure out what love looks like. God showed us at Calvary. He sent his Son to die for our sins. Since God loved us like this, we are under obligation to love others. When we love others, God lives in us. Fires of God burn low when we refuse to love others.

The church at Ephesus was warned that if they did not return to love, their influence would be removed. They had worked hard, showed patience, did not tolerate evil people,

had suffered for Christ's sake, but one thing was missing—
they had lost the love that had characterized them when they
first came into Christ. It is that important.

Keep on being hospitable

First-century Christians did not have a *Travelers Inn*.
They had to depend on the hospitality of others to provide
a safe place when they traveled. Social conditions made hospitality a necessity. It seems some were afraid to open their
houses to strangers. It always carried a risk. The author tried
to encourage them with the thought that they might be
entertaining angels and not be aware of it when they were
hospitable.

Keep on caring for one another

Those who were imprisoned for their faith deserve the
love and support of other Christians. Those who were suffering for their faith deserve the same. The church should
enter into their hardships as if they themselves were there
with them. Out of mind could lead to out of sympathy.

Andrei Sakharov estimated that today there were at
least two thousand people in Russia imprisoned for their
faith. Scripture may not have a lot of meaning to us here in
America, but around the world, it is as up-to-date as their
next breath.

Another group that I would include here is the elderly.
Many of them are in prison without bars. They are isolated
and ignored. When I retired, I went to work with an agency
named Tennessee Agency for Aging. I worked with the elderly
in Upper Tennessee. They are the most ignored people in our
community. I discovered that even churches had forgotten
them when they could no longer serve. One client told me

that she had taught in the Sunday school of her church for forty years, but now that she could not attend, they had forgotten her. They need our care. A card, a letter, prayer, or a phone call would brighten their day. We need to care for this group in our community.

Keep on being faithful to marriage vows

In every congregation there are people we know who are breaking up or have broken up their marriage. Many times, it is because one of the partners have been unfaithful to their vow to be faithful till death. We forget that there is a warning here. God will judge us.

Our society is saturated with television programs that promote or encourage unfaithfulness. It seems that they would not have material for their production if they do not promote unfaithfulness in the marriage relationship.

Good marriages require hard work. It needs to begin when our children are very young. We need to give them a good example to pattern their future lives. My wife and I have been married for sixty-nine years this year, and we know the value of hard work in marriage.

Keep on avoiding greed

Greed is selfishness gone amok. It is selfishness that desires beyond reason. It basically indicates a lack of trust in God's ability to help us in time of need. When we think greed, we usually think money. It is not money but the love of money that is the root of so much evil in our society. We see this play out in daily news reports. There are people who give no thought to destroying lives all because for the love of money.

Greed is also pictured in lottery. It indicates that we are discontented with what we have in the material world. Things and happiness do not necessarily go together. Some of the most unhappy people in this world are those who have the most material things.

There is a difference between greed and ambition. Greed is selfishness beyond reason while ambition is the desire to succeed in the task God has given us to do. Success enters into it, but there is more involved than just personal success. We want to give our best whatever our task.

Keep on working with spiritual leaders

Those who have already died can inspire us by way they lived their lives. There are those who are presently with us that need our support. They have dedicated their lives to the welfare of the church. When we work cooperatively with them, they do their work with joy. When we do not work with them; they do their work with grief.

Keep on clinging to Jesus

"Jesus Christ, the same yesterday, today, and forever." Hebrews 13:8 comes between verses seven and nine. Verse seven commends the faithful, and verse nine condemns false teaching. Why leave Jesus, who never changes, to follow a strange teaching that does not help us?

Verses nine through twelve are difficult verses for us to understand. The general agreement may be stated thus: "Do not be carried away by the fascination with teaching that are foreign to the Christianity you have been taught."

The first readers knew what was meant and seems to have given in to this strange teaching. It had to do with food. Evidently there were those who were teaching that certain foods strengthen the heart (probably spiritually). But the author tells them that food do not help us spiritually. God's grace is all we need.

We must take care that we do not have some strange teaching. As a youth, growing up in a rural community, I got the impression that if I didn't do certain activities, then I was being a good Christian. I know now that all the "don't do" in the world does not make me a Christian. We need to major on the "dos" of our faith. Jesus told us, "whoever hears these sayings of mine and *does* them…"

Keep on having a bold faith

"The Lord is my helper; I will not fear. What shall man do to me?" This does not occur in our Old Testament in the form here. Perhaps it refers to Deuteronomy 31:6, 8. It is true wherever the author found it. The Lord is our helper. Jesus made the ultimate sacrifice for us. We don't sacrifice animals, but we join him by making a sacrifice of praise to God. We can boldly join him in sharing his shame of the cross. We can give a sacrifice of time, money, and abilities to witness to the truth of Christianity.

Keep on praying

"I appeal to you" is an indication that he could not count with certainty on a favorable hearing. He asks them to pray for him that he might soon be with them. He evidently stood close to them. When he goes from the plural to the singular (18), he includes others.

Timothy must have been imprisoned at some time in the past, but we know nothing of the circumstance. He says that they must know that Timothy has been released from prison. He hopes to have him with him when he comes to visit them.

We need each other. We need the prayers of other Christians. Sometimes the best gift we can bring is a prayer to God for others. When we pray for others, we take our minds off ourself. No one can work for God unaided and unsupported.

John Fawcett said it well: "Before our Father's throne, we pour out ardent prayers. *Our fears, our hope, our aims are one*, our comfort and our cares."

About the Author

At the time of this writing, Edward Scarbrough was nine-ty-two years old and has been married for sixty-nine years. He preached his first sermon in 1949, began his first pastorate in 1952, and dedicated his life to working with churches that needed help. In the process, he pastored four churches, one of them twice, both before and after seminary. One small church started with eighteen in attendance and, after seven years, averaged around 140. He has also served several churches in their area as an interim pastor multiple times. To support his family, Edward taught in public schools and eventually became a principal of a large county high school. He holds a master's degree in administration and supervision and, for the last five years of his tenure, served as regional director of the Academy of School Leaders for the State Department of Education. He doesn't consider himself an authority in sermon preparation, but he has been building sermons for at least seventy years, using notes he has collected as he read through the Scripture. He retired from preaching at eighty years of age due to health reasons but still maintains a study in his home and spends time daily studying Scripture.

When again working his way through Hebrews, he began to record snippets that would lead to one or more sermons from each chapter. If someone can profit from his work, he says, then he would be satisfied.

* 9 7 9 8 8 9 1 3 0 3 4 9 2 *